Three Wise Birds

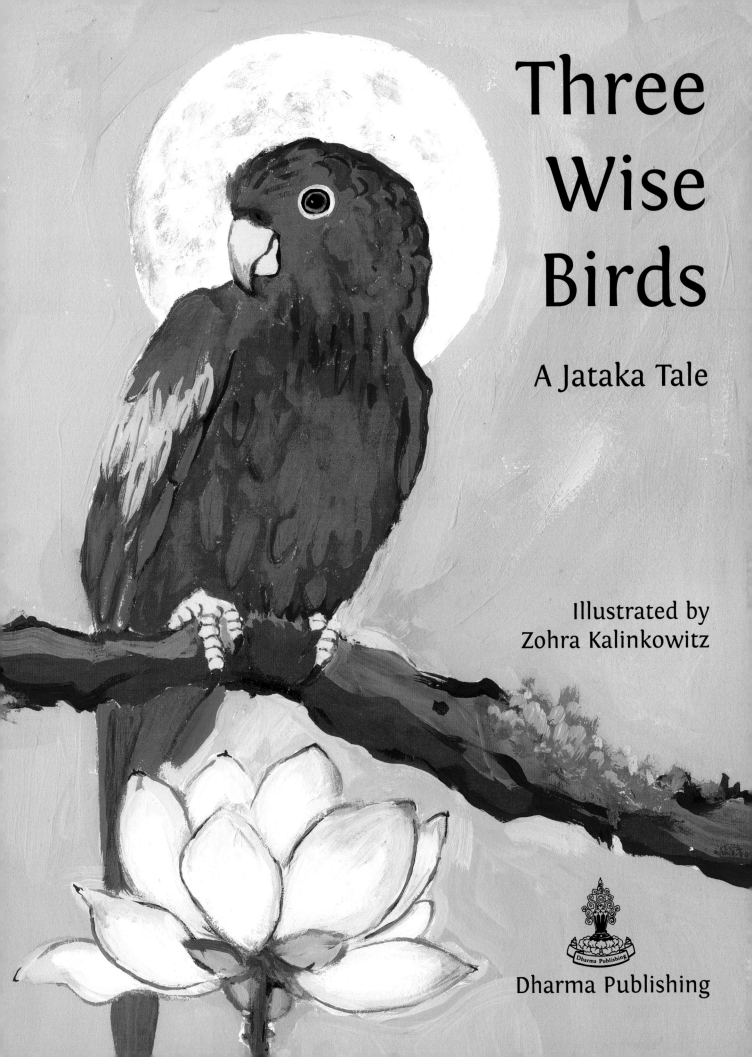

Three
Wise
Birds

A Jataka Tale

Illustrated by
Zohra Kalinkowitz

Dharma Publishing

Jataka Tales Series

Third edition 2009, revised and augmented with
guidance for parents and teachers.
Cover design by Kando Dorsey.

Printed on acid-free paper

Printed in the USA by Dharma Press, 35788 Hauser Bridge Rd.,
Cazadero, California 95421.

9   8   7   6   5   4   3   2   1

Text based on the Tesakuna Jataka, adapted by
the Dharma Publishing staff for the first edition published in 1976.
Library of Congress Control Number: 2009940426

ISBN 978-089800-521-9

www.dharmapublishing.com

Dedicated to children everywhere

Once there lived in India a king who had a palace filled with treasures gathered from far and wide. But the king was not happy. Although he had plenty of gold, and rooms full of costly and rare possessions, he was not satisfied. He felt his life was not complete because he had no children.

One day the king went to the royal park together with some courtiers and attendants. There he walked beside sparkling waterfalls, listened to soft breezes humming through the leaves, and looked into cool, deep ponds filled with lotus blossoms of every color. His spirits brightened, but still he was not content.

At midday the king lay down to rest at the foot of a sal tree and gazed up through the green canopy of leaves. High up in the branches, an unusual bird's nest caught his eye. As soon as the king saw the nest he knew he wanted to have it. He called to one of his attendants, "Climb the tree and bring me that nest!"

The man climbed up to the nest and found three eggs. "Be careful!" warned the king. He took a white silk scarf from his neck, folded it and placed it into a golden case shining with jewels. Handing the case to the attendant in the tree, he said, "Pick the eggs up gently and place them in this case."

When the eggs were nestled safely in the precious case, the king questioned his courtiers, "What kind of bird might these eggs belong to?"

"We do not know," they answered. "Perhaps the woodsmen can tell us."

The king sent for the woodsmen. "Pray, to which birds do these eggs belong?"

"Your majesty," they said, "these eggs belong to three completely different birds! One egg is an owl's, one is a mynah's, and one is a parrot's."

The king was astonished. "Hmmm!" he said. "How odd! Can the eggs of three different birds hatch in one nest? I doubt it."

But the woodsmen answered, "What is kept with care and safe from fear, will grow and thrive for many a year."

As the king heard these words, an idea came to him. To the surprise of everyone, he held up the golden case with the three eggs and proclaimed: "Please consider these three birds as my own children!"

He commanded three of his most loyal courtiers to watch over the eggs until they hatched.

The courtiers did as the king asked. Before long, the first bird came out of its shell. It was the owl. The courtier who had been caring for this egg hurried to the king, saying, "Sire, sire! A son has been born to you from the wise owl's egg!"

The king was delighted with the news. "Name my newborn son Vessantara," he said. "Care for him as you would care for me."

Just a few days later, the mynah bird was hatched. The courtier who had been caring for the egg hurried to the king. "Sire, sire!" he cried. "A daughter has been born to you!" The king was delighted with the news and named her Kundalini. "Care for her as you would care for me," he told the second courtier.

Finally, the golden egg of the parrot was hatched. The third courtier knelt before the king, saying, "Sire! You have another son to grace your royal family."

Filled with joy, the king proclaimed, "We will call my youngest son Jambuka, and hold a festival in his name. Everyone will come to celebrate."
He sent the courtier on his way, saying, "Care for my son as you would care for me."

The three young birds were raised in the palace as if they were the king's own children. Whenever the king spoke of the birds he always called them "my sons" and "my daughter." He talked to them every day.

One day the king overheard some of his courtiers gossiping. "Look how silly our king is acting," said one. "He goes about speaking to the birds as if they were human. Imagine that!" And another said, "As if our little birds could understand one word he says. Could he be losing his mind?"

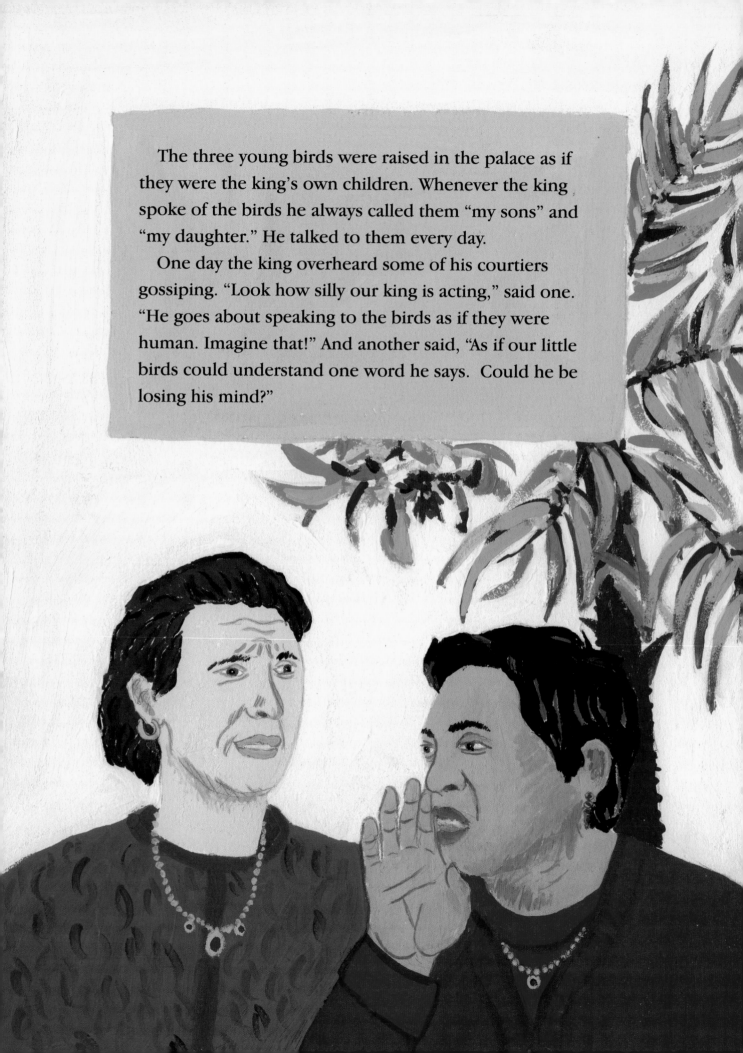

The king thought to himself: "They have no idea how wise my beloved children are! I must help them to see." He decided to assemble his people and, in front of the crowd, to put a question to each of the birds. "That will open my people's eyes," he thought.

The king ordered three grand pavilions to be erected in the palace courtyard. The next morning he seated himself in the first pavilion, surrounded by his courtiers and attendants. He ordered a drum to be beaten through the city streets to proclaim an important occasion.

The sound of drumbeats boomed through the town, and soon a crowd gathered from all around. "What is going on?" people asked as they squeezed through the palace gates. "It must be something terribly important!" Parents put their children on their shoulders so they could see what was happening in the palace yard.

When all had settled down, the king called for
the first of his children to be brought in. With great
ceremony the owl Vessantara was placed upon a
golden stool. With glistening feathers and pointed
beak, he waited. Then the king spoke to him,
    "My son, pray tell me, and may you be blessed,
To follow what rule for a king would be best?"
    Leaving the golden stool and jumping on his
father's knee, Vessantara answered:
        "I urge you kindly, father dear,
        make sure your path in life is clear.
        A king must set aside jealousy and greed.
        For he who fails to rule himself,
        will also surely fail to lead.

Be generous, father, never jealous
and spend your efforts on good things.
Blessings from the heaven realms
will crown you then a worthy king."

   The crowd shouted and applauded. "Amazing!" some exclaimed. "Not only can this owl speak, but also his words are wise and true. Our king is blessed to have such a fine son!"

   And the king rewarded the owl Vessantara with the post of general of the royal army.

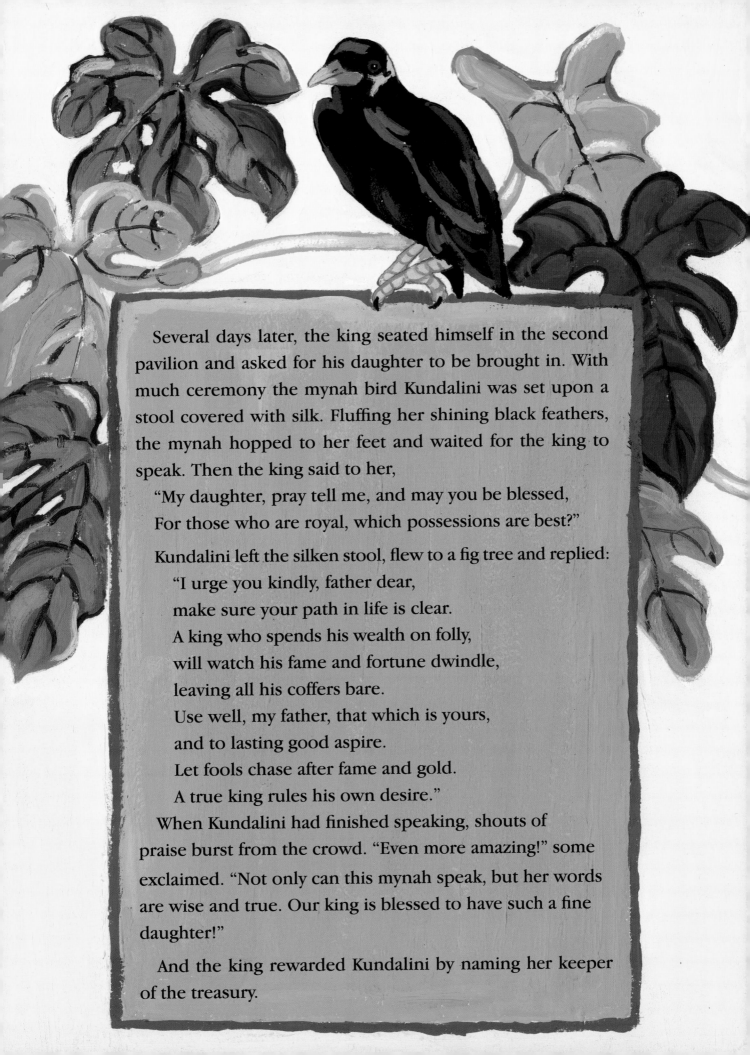

Several days later, the king seated himself in the second pavilion and asked for his daughter to be brought in. With much ceremony the mynah bird Kundalini was set upon a stool covered with silk. Fluffing her shining black feathers, the mynah hopped to her feet and waited for the king to speak. Then the king said to her,

"My daughter, pray tell me, and may you be blessed,
For those who are royal, which possessions are best?"

Kundalini left the silken stool, flew to a fig tree and replied:

"I urge you kindly, father dear,
make sure your path in life is clear.
A king who spends his wealth on folly,
will watch his fame and fortune dwindle,
leaving all his coffers bare.
Use well, my father, that which is yours,
and to lasting good aspire.
Let fools chase after fame and gold.
A true king rules his own desire."

When Kundalini had finished speaking, shouts of praise burst from the crowd. "Even more amazing!" some exclaimed. "Not only can this mynah speak, but her words are wise and true. Our king is blessed to have such a fine daughter!"

And the king rewarded Kundalini by naming her keeper of the treasury.

Several days later the king took his seat in the third pavilion and asked for Jambuka, the youngest of the royal birds, to be brought in. What a splendid parrot he was, radiant in a rainbow of many colors and feathered crown!

Arranging his feathers and shining his beak, Jambuka waited for his turn to speak. Then the king said:

"Can you tell us, Jambuka, and may you be blessed, for a king, what kind of power is best?"

Jambuka replied respectfully,

"I urge you kindly, father dear,
make sure your path in life
is clear.

"The power to know, to see and to be wise,
is the highest power one can realize.
When the light of wisdom shines like the sun,
all other powers can be won.
A king with wisdom at his side,
free from foolishness and pride,
has the power to see what is true
and know in life what he must do.
My father, listen to this advice:
Live an ordered, simple life.
Rule with wisdom and you shall see
how happy a worthy king can be."

When Jambuka had spoken, the crowd shouted with applause and admiration. "Truly the parrot teaches with the charm of a Buddha," they said.

And the king bestowed upon Jambuka the office of commander-in-chief.

From that day on, the three wise birds were
honored in the palace and in town, and they
gave advice on important matters of all kinds.
As for the king, he took to heart the words of his
three children. He lived simply, served his people
well and became rich in wisdom.

When the king had grown old, he told his
counselors that after his death, Jambuka was to
become the next king. But when Jambuka heard
this, he said,

"Now that your counselors have grown in
wisdom, they are well prepared to rule. I have
no need of a kingdom."

Then Jambuka gave the people a golden plate with the three birds' teachings engraved upon it. He bid the king farewell and disappeared into the forest.

Following the teachings of the three wise birds, the people and their leaders enjoyed many years of peace and prosperity.

PARENTS AND TEACHERS CORNER

The Jataka Tales nurture in readers young and old an appreciation for values shared by all the world's great traditions. Read aloud, performed and studied for centuries, they communicate universal values such as kindness, forgiveness, compassion, humility, courage, honesty and patience. You can bring these stories alive through the suggestions on these pages. Actively engaging with the stories creates a bridge to the children in your life and opens a dialogue about what brings joy, stability and caring.

Three Wise Birds

A king discovers three unusual eggs, and since he is childless, he raises the young birds as if they were his children. To dispel the doubts of his people, the king has the birds display their wisdom. Each bird's wise counsel helps the king govern fairly until he is very old, and the birds are honored and heeded by all people.

Key Values
Heeding advice
Leadership
Ruling oneself

Bringing the story to life

Engage the children by saying, "In this story a king views three birds: a parrot, a mynah bird and an owl, as his children. His people are upset with him. Let's read to find out what happens."

- What does the king discover that makes him content?
- How does the king want the birds cared for?
- Why do the people doubt their king?
- Have you ever heard of talking birds? What do these three birds say to the king?
- Why do the people change their minds and decide that each bird is a worthy royal child?
- What kind of advice does the last bird, the parrot, give the king?
- Why doesn't the wise parrot want to become king? What happens to the people and their leaders?

Discussion topics and questions can be modified depending on the child's age.

Teaching values through play

Follow up on the storytelling with creative activities that explore the characters and values and appeal to the five senses.

- Have the children construct and decorate character masks for the king, parrot, owl, and mynah bird; or they can cut out and color a single feather for each bird, and a crown for the king. In their own clothes they can take turns as the king's subjects and counselors. The birds can each give their advice to the king. The children can decide at which point the people come to trust the birds. Have them talk about what each bird might be like based on the kind of advice they give.

- In their masks or holding their feathers, children can fly like their particular bird and give that bird's call; then pick one key word of advice from each bird and make that part of the bird's call. For example, the parrot could say "wisdom shines like the sun" as he flies and also when he lands and perches.

- Have the children retell the story in their own words from the point of view of one of the birds.

Active reading

- Before children can read, they enjoy storytelling and love growing familiar with the characters and drawings. You can show them the pictures and tell the story in your own words with characteristic voices for the birds and the king.

- Display the key values on the refrigerator or a bulletin board – at child's eye level – and refer to them in your daily interactions.

- Integrate the wisdom of this story into challenging situations: when two children disagree or one child dominates another, ask, "What would the parrot say to you here?" When someone has trouble sharing, remind him or her of the owl's advice about setting aside jealousy and greed.

- Talk about the story with your child while engaged in daily activities like cooking, taking

care of a pet, or driving. Over dinner you could start a discussion about what makes a good leader. Think of each bird's recommendation in relation to current local, national and world leaders.

- If the children have pets, you can compare the care for the eggs to the children's care of the animal they love. Or you can find out about care of birds by looking online at the efforts of organizations such as the World Bird Sanctuary.

- You can listen online to the call of many birds.

Names and places

- **Sal tree**: a tree found in southern Asia that is an important source of hardwood timber.
- **Owl**: a mostly nocturnal bird of prey, associated with wisdom and prosperity.
- **Mynah**: a gregarious bird, typically with a dark plumage, and some imitative skills.
- **Parrot**: considered to be one of the most intelligent birds, able to imitate human voices.

We are grateful for the opportunity to offer these Jataka Tales to you. May they inspire fresh insight into the dynamics of human relationships and may understanding grow with each reading.

This adaptation of a Jataka Tale is for children aged five to ten

JATAKA TALES SERIES